YOU CHOOSE
BOOKS™

BUILDING THE
Empire State
BUILDING

An Interactive Engineering Adventure

by Allison Lassieur

Consultant:
Karen C. Chou, PhD., P.E., F.ASCE
Clinical Professor, Department of Civil & Environmental Engineering
Northwestern University

D0066714

CAPSTONE PRESS
a capstone imprint

You Choose Books are published by Capstone Press,
1710 Roe Crest Drive, North Mankato, Minnesota 56003
www.capstonepub.com

Library of Congress Cataloging-in-Publication Data
Lassieur, Allison, author.
 Building the Empire State Building : an interactive engineering adventure / by Allison Lassieur.
  pages cm.—(You choose. Engineering marvels)
  Summary: "Explores various perspectives on the process of building the Empire State Building.
The reader's choices reveal the historical details"—Provided by publisher.
 Includes bibliographical references and index.
 ISBN 978-1-4914-0400-3 (library binding)
 ISBN 978-1-4914-0405-8 (paperback)
 ISBN 978-1-4914-0409-6 (ebook PDF)
1. Empire State Building (New York, N.Y.)—Design and construction—History—Juvenile
literature. 2. Building, Iron and steel—History—Juvenile literature. 3. Architecture—New York
(State)—New York—Juvenile literature. 4. New York (N.Y.)—History—1898-1951—Juvenile
literature. I. Title.
TH149.L37 2015
974.7'1—dc23   2013047697

Editorial Credits

Adrian Vigliano, editor; Veronica Scott, designer; Wanda Winch, media researcher; Laura Manthe,
production specialist

Photo Credits

BlueprintPlace, 33; Corbis, 41, Bettmann, 10, 42, 66, 75, 82, 85, 87, 96, 105, Underwood &
Underwood, 12, 20; Getty Images Inc: Archive Photos/Lionel Green, 99, George Eastman House/
Lewis W. Hine, 49, 54, 59, 62, 65, 76, Hulton Archive/FPG, 70, Keystone-France/Gamma-
Keystone, 16, The New York Historical Society/Frank M. Ingalls, 25, Transcendental Graphics,
100; Library of Congress: Prints and Photographs Division, cover, 6; Shutterstock: alekup, grunge
blueprint design, iofoto, cover (inset), Sociologas, graph paper design

Printed in Canada.
032014   008086FRF14

TABLE OF CONTENTS

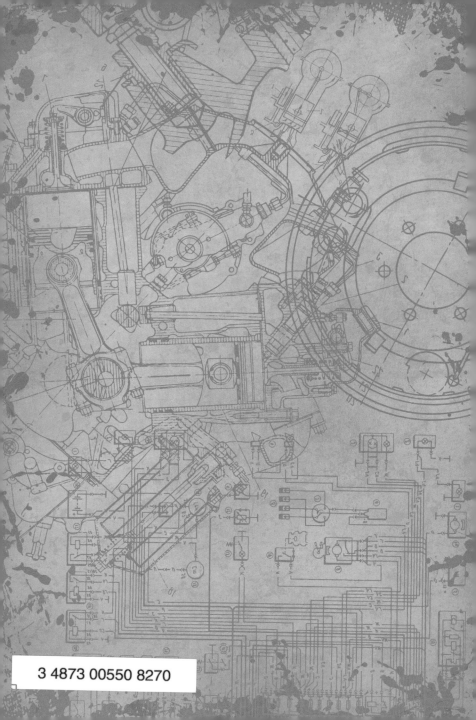

About Your Adventure

The Empire State Building was the tallest building in the world when it was completed. It remains one of the most famous structures in the United States. Built during the hard times of the Great Depression, it became a symbol of hope for the country.

In this book you'll explore how the choices people made meant the difference between success and failure. The events you'll experience happened to real people.

Chapter One sets the scene. Then you choose which path to read. Follow the directions at the bottom of each page. The choices you make will change your outcome. After you finish one path, go back and read the others for new perspectives and more adventures.

YOU CHOOSE the path you take through history.

Standing at 1,250 feet, the Empire State Building became the tallest skyscraper in the world in 1931. Its design is said to have been largely based on the shape of a pencil.

RACE TO THE SKY

It was the tallest structure on Earth. Some people called it the "Eighth Wonder of the World." The Empire State Building was a marvel of architecture and technology when it was finished in 1931.

This grand building was thought up during a time of big ideas. The 1920s were a period of excitement. Jobs were plentiful in the United States, and almost everyone seemed to have enough money.

Turn the page.

During the "Roaring Twenties" wealthy Americans made their fortunes in businesses such as railroads, oil, and automobiles. After years of making money, many of these individuals began looking for new challenges. For some, the perfect challenge was competing to build the world's tallest building.

Many notable people wanted to be a part of the great New York skyscraper race. Rich businessmen began pouring millions of dollars into building projects.

One of the first great skyscraper projects began when millionaire Frank W. Woolworth paid cash to finance the construction of the Woolworth Building. The 60-story Woolworth Building became famous when it was completed in 1913. It remained the tallest building in the world for the next 17 years.

The Metropolitan Life North Building was designed to break height records at 100 stories tall. But financial problems forced construction to stop at floor 29.

With 77 stories the Chrysler Building became the world's tallest when it was finished in 1930. But a new challenger, the Empire State Building, would soon rise even higher.

The Empire State was the tallest and the grandest skyscraper the world had ever seen. Its clean, modern lines were designed according to the Art Deco style. The city—and the whole country—was proud of the new building when it was finished in 1931.

Turn the page.

The Great Depression caused many people to struggle to feed their families. In the scene above, unemployed New Yorkers in 1930 wait to receive food from a charitable organization.

But major economic changes had occurred by 1931. The fun, carefree days of the 1920s had come to an end. In October 1929 the stock market crashed, sending the country into the Great Depression. Millions of people lost their jobs. There wasn't much to be hopeful about. The Empire State Building was one of the few construction projects that went on after the crash. People saw it as a sign that things were going to get better.

You can experience the danger, struggle, and excitement of being part of the construction of the world's tallest building. There are many jobs available, and each one is important to the project's success.

To be a young architect designing the Empire State Building, turn to page 13.

To be a riveter from Brooklyn, working high in the steel, turn to page 43.

To be a water boy at the end of construction, turn to page 67.

New York's Times Square was a bright, noisy, and vibrant place to be in the 1920s.

CHAPTER 2

A BIG IDEA

The 1920s is an exciting decade to live in New York City. With the end of World War I in 1918, the world is ready to have some fun. New York City seems to be the center of attention. The streets fill with a new music called jazz. At night the city glows with electric lights.

By 1929 almost 6 million people live in New York, and you are one of them. You came here to go to Columbia University Graduate School of Architecture, the best architecture school in the country. After graduation you decided to stay. New York is the place to be.

13

Turn the page.

You have a big dream: to design tall buildings. That's why you pursued a job with the best architecture firm in town, Shreve, Lamb, and Harmon. They are famous in New York for their tall buildings. You got a job with them, and you feel lucky to be a part of the team.

The firm's big project is a 50-story building. It won't be the world's tallest, but it will be a skyscraper. When you arrive at the office, there is a message waiting for you. It informs you that the team is meeting with some investors about the new project.

The meeting room is more chaotic than you've ever seen before. Everyone is talking at once. Mr. Lamb tells everyone to quiet down and waves you to a seat. A stranger is seated next to him.

"Everyone, this is John J. Raskob," Mr. Lamb says. You recognize Raskob as one of the richest businessmen in New York. He is the former head of General Motors, one of the biggest car companies. You're not sure why he is here. He doesn't have anything to do with the 50-story building project.

Mr. Lamb has some bad news. The 50-story project has been cancelled. The deal to buy the land for the building has fallen through. Mr. Lamb is smiling, though. He's got more news. Mr. Raskob and some other men bought the land. They want to build a different skyscraper, and they want your firm to design it.

"Will it be the world's tallest building?" you ask hopefully.

15

Turn the page.

Mr. Raskob pulls out a pencil. He holds it, point up, and looks at Mr. Lamb. "Bill, how high can you make it so that it won't fall down?"

Raskob goes on to tell the group that he wants this skyscraper to beat the Chrysler Building, which is currently being constructed. It is clear that this will be a competition to see who can build the taller skyscraper.

By the summer of 1929 construction on the Chrysler Building was well underway.

There is only one problem. The architects behind the Chrysler Building are keeping their plans a secret. No one knows how high the Chrysler Building will be. Your firm will have to guess how high the Chrysler will be, then design something even taller.

The meeting breaks up and everyone heads back to the office. As you leave you hear Mr. Raskob mention that one of his partners, former governor of New York Al Smith, is about to hold a press conference. He'll be giving some details about this new project. Going to the press conference could be a useful way to gather more information. But you can't wait to get back to your desk and work on ideas for the new building.

To listen to Al Smith, turn to page 18.

To go back to your office, turn to page 20.

Al Smith has called the press to his rooms at the Hotel Biltmore, near Grand Central station. The room is crowded with reporters pushing one another for the best view of the former governor. When he begins to talk everyone gets quiet.

"I'm the president of a new company," he says. "It's called the Empire State Building Corporation. And I'm pleased to announce that we're going to build the world's tallest building!"

He continues by saying the building will be over 1,000 feet high. It will have 80 stories of office space. This amazing building will be built on 2 acres of land in midtown Manhattan, where the old Waldorf-Astoria hotel now stands.

The reporters begin firing questions at the former governor.

"Why did you choose the old Waldorf-Astoria site?" one shouts.

Smith chuckles. "Have you ever been down there?" he asks. "It's one of the busiest areas in the city! Buses pass right by the site, and subway stops are only a short walk away. The best stores in Manhattan, such as Macy's, the world's largest department store, are nearby. It's the perfect place for an office building."

Mr. Smith's excitement rubs off on you and everyone else in the room. You head back to the office, ready to get started.

Turn to page 20.

Everyone is buzzing with excitement. Ideas for the world's tallest building seem to tumble out of your pencil as you draw design after design. Everyone works hard for days, hoping to come up with the best idea.

Some Empire State Building architects set up temporary desks in the main dining room of the Waldorf-Astoria before it was torn down.

One good thing about the Waldorf-Astoria site is how big it is. The 2-acre lot is twice as large as most building sites in the city. That means the new skyscraper can be huge. You know that once you finish your designs, Mr. Lamb and Mr. Shreve will want to see them.

You have a lot of respect for both of your bosses. Mr. Lamb studied architecture in Paris. He is one of the best designers in the city.
Mr. Shreve once taught architecture at Cornell University. He is the best at running a job and making sure a project stays on time and on budget. Mr. Lamb will give you good suggestions about your design. Mr. Shreve can tell you if your design is practical, and how much it would cost.

To show your ideas to Mr. Lamb, turn to page 22.
To show your ideas to Mr. Shreve, turn to page 36.

Mr. Lamb nods approvingly. He thinks you've made a good start. But he reminds you of the zoning law in New York about tall buildings. This law states that buildings can't rise straight up from the sidewalk, as your designs do. If all buildings did that, then it would be more difficult for sunlight to get to the ground.

The law says that after 150 feet, every tall building has to "step back" as it gets higher. That would make the skyscraper narrower as it got taller to allow light and air to get to the street. He encourages you to think about a design that is new and fresh, but will still follow the law.

Mr. Lamb says that they are going to choose the contractors who will handle all of the construction for the project. You can come along to the meeting, or you can show your ideas to Mr. Shreve.

To help choose the contractors, go to page 23.

To show your plan to Mr. Shreve, turn to page 36.

Al Smith and the rest of the Empire State Building Corporation are at the meeting. Mr. Lamb, Mr. Shreve, and Mr. Harmon are also there. One by one the best contractors in the city make presentations. Finally the last contractor comes in, Starrett Brothers. Al Smith greets them, saying, "Well, what have you got to say for yourselves?"

Paul Starrett says he is going to prove that he and his brother are the best contractors for the job. As you wonder how he's going to do that, he rattles off a list of accomplishments. They are the only contractors who are also trained architects. This year, his company built the 70-story Bank of Manhattan Trust Building at 40 Wall Street, which was in the race with the Chrysler Building as the world's tallest. Most importantly, they are known for their speed. The 40 Wall Street building went up in only 11 months.

Turn the page.

"How much equipment do you have?"
Mr. Smith asks.

Paul Starrett shocks you with his answer. "Not a thing. Not even a pick and shovel." You look around the room. Everyone looks as surprised as you feel. Then Starrett says, "Gentlemen, this building of yours is going to present unusual problems. Ordinary building equipment won't be worth a thing on it. We'll buy new stuff, fitted for the job, and at the end, sell it and credit you with the difference. It costs less than renting secondhand stuff, and it's more efficient."

He also promises to tear down the Waldorf-Astoria and finish the construction in 18 months. *That's impossible*, you think.

After Paul Starrett leaves, the group talks about the presentations. Starrett certainly made a big impression. You sit back, trying to decide whether it would be smarter to go with one of the other, more traditional contractors. Then again, maybe Starrett can deliver on his promises. Then Mr. Lamb calls for quiet in the room. He wants to hear your opinion.

The Waldorf-Astoria set a new standard for quality. It offered luxurious features at a time when hotels catered mostly to lower classes.

To argue for Starrett Brothers, turn to page 26.

To argue for one of the other contractors, turn to page 37.

You say that you like Paul Starrett's confidence and ambition. You acknowledge that his fee, $600,000, is high, but it's a worthwhile investment if he can finish the job in 18 months. The others agree with you.

The next few weeks are a flurry of meetings with the owners, architects, and builders. It is important that everyone works together to plan the entire project. As Mr. Shreve said to you more than once, keeping everyone on the same page helps avoid design mistakes. It also makes the construction run smoothly, and catches problems early.

One day Mr. Lamb calls a meeting. The group has come up with guidelines for the building. No space in the whole building can be more than 28 feet wide, from window to hallway. The outside of the building will be made of limestone. The whole building has to be finished by May 1, 1931, which is a year and six months from now. And the project must stay under budget.

Then he shares the good news: the guidelines allow for there to be as many stories as possible. Now it's time to come up with the final design.

To work on the inside space design, turn to page 28.

To work on the height design, turn to page 30.

Mr. Lamb demands that every inside space in the building must be flooded with sunlight. But office buildings need other features such as stairways, elevators, and bathrooms. In most buildings these things are on the sides or corners of the building. But they block sunlight to parts of each floor.

You struggle with this problem for days. Then suddenly the answer comes to you. Put all the elevators and bathrooms in the middle! Quickly you sketch out your idea and show it to Mr. Lamb.

He points out that the floors get narrower as the building gets higher. The highest offices won't have 28 feet between the windows and the hallways. You explain that the offices will be smaller, but they will be brighter and quieter. The views will be magnificent. The owners can charge more to rent those spaces, even though they're smaller.

Mr. Lamb is impressed. Instead of working from the bottom up, you designed the highest offices first and worked down. "That's top-down design," Mr. Lamb says. He tells you that the next two priorities are designing the steel structure and working on the building's height.

To work on the height design, turn to page 30.

To work on the steel structure design, turn to page 32.

How high can the world's tallest building be? At first you design a building with more than 100 floors. But then you learn that the owners don't have enough money to build that high. They can only afford about 85 floors. That is still taller than 40 Wall Street, which is now the tallest building. It has only 72 stories. When you show your ideas to Mr. Shreve, he nods in approval.

"Also think about the elevators," he says. "The height of the building also depends on how good the elevators are." He invites you to meet with the builders about the elevators.

Skyscrapers would not be possible without the invention of the elevator. The key for this project is to design one that will move many people faster than any other elevator. After many meetings with the Otis Elevator Company, you emerge with the design for a fast elevator system. The limit of the new elevator system is about 80 floors. Above that, smaller elevators will take people to the highest floors. You are thrilled when the new design is approved.

You know that Mr. Lamb needs someone to work on the building's steel structure design. You've also heard that work on the exterior design is about to begin.

To design the steel structure, turn to page 32.
To work on the exterior, turn to page 34.

As you begin work on the steel structure design, you think about what you learned in architecture school. In the past, buildings had a skeleton of cast iron. Cast iron is heavy. It doesn't bend or move well in the wind. These are reasons buildings with a cast-iron structure could not rise very high. Steel is different. It is stronger and more flexible than cast iron. It can bend and move in the wind. That is very important for a tall building. Tall buildings have to move a little in the wind or they will break.

Together you and Mr. Lamb design a three-dimensional steel skeleton for the Empire State Building. This skeleton will hold all the weight of the building. The walls will hang on the steel skeleton. This will let you create any kind of walls and windows you want. The windows will let in plenty of light and air to every floor.

Mr. Lamb mentions that demolition has started on the Waldorf-Astoria hotel. You could go watch the old building come down. Or you can stay and work on more ideas.

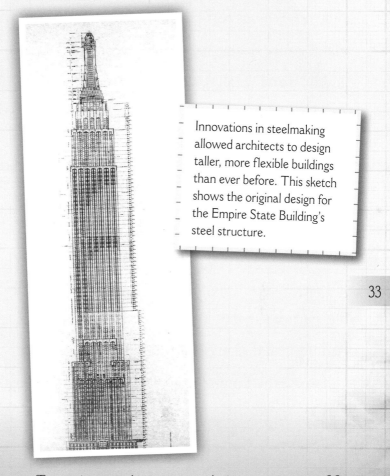

Innovations in steelmaking allowed architects to design taller, more flexible buildings than ever before. This sketch shows the original design for the Empire State Building's steel structure.

33

To continue working on your design, turn to page 38.

To take a break and watch the demolition, turn to page 40.

Keep things simple—that's what all the architects you've known have drilled into your head. Most buildings have decorations on the outside, like sculptures, buttresses, and carvings. But those things cost money, and Mr. Shreve is making sure this project stays on budget. You and he sketch a tall tower, elegant and simple. You imagine long bands of simple, beautifully cut limestone for the outside of the building.

The 6,400 windows are simple too. Most building windows are set deep inside the walls. But Mr. Shreve wants the windows even with the outside wall. This design makes the windows look like part of the wall itself. You've never seen that curtain-wall design before, and it's impressive. It will make the Empire State Building look modern.

Mr. Shreve explains that designing the walls and the windows this way will make construction go much faster. It will also mean the building will use 75 percent less stone than other skyscrapers.

Everyone is pleased with the design. Now you're ready to get to work designing the inside of the building. But then Mr. Shreve says that there's still time to see the Waldorf-Astoria come down. It's your last chance to catch a glimpse of the demolition. Soon the Empire State Building will rise in its place.

To work on interior designs, turn to page 38.

To watch the demolition, turn to page 40.

Mr. Shreve frowns as he looks at your designs. He points out that the materials you want to use are very expensive. You argue that they are the best materials for your design.

"This might be the world's tallest building, but it won't be the world's most expensive!" he says. He also tells you that the owners want the building finished by May 1, 1931.

"That's less than two years away!" you gasp. "There's no way the world's tallest building can go up that fast."

"If you think that way," he says, "then maybe you aren't the right person for this project." Your heart sinks. He says you can work on another project, but your dream is crushed. Sadly you clean out your desk and leave for good.

THE END

To follow another path, turn to page 11.
To read the conclusion, turn to page 101.

You decide that the first contractor is a safer bet, and say so. Everyone listens politely, but it's clear that no one else agrees. They all want Starrett Brothers. You argue that Paul Starrett wants $600,000, far more than any of the others asked for.

"There is no way anyone can build the world's tallest building in only 18 months!" you say.

Mr. Lamb frowns, but you keep arguing. The more you argue, the more convinced you are that your opinion is right. Finally Mr. Shreve pulls you aside. They've made their decision, and it's going to be Starrett Brothers. By that time, you're so angry that you quit on the spot, storming out of the room. *There will be other skyscrapers*, you think angrily.

THE END

To follow another path, turn to page 11.
To read the conclusion, turn to page 101.

You have plenty of ideas for the lobby of the Empire State Building. It should be simple, like the rest of the building. But the materials should be luxurious. There aren't any carvings or decorations on the elegant marble walls. You want the natural beauty of the marble to shine. You design a large aluminum and gold mural that shows the Empire State Building in all its glory. You sketch plans for another beautiful mural of starbursts on the ceiling made of canvas, aluminum, and gold.

You even have ideas for the lights and other fixtures. They should be in the Art Deco style, which is very popular. Art Deco style is filled with strong shapes and colors with a clean, modern look.

It's your best design yet, and everyone loves it. Mr. Lamb congratulates you on a job well done. Your ideas are put into the final design of the building.

On your way home it finally hits you. You are an architect, and you are working on the world's tallest building! The building is going to be famous. You might be famous someday too. Eventually you begin working on different buildings, but you keep a close eye on the Empire State Building's construction. As the building rises up above New York's skyline, you're proud to have been a part of such an innovative project.

THE END

To follow another path, turn to page 11.
To read the conclusion, turn to page 101.

Demolition is loud, dirty, and exciting. Strings of electric lights crisscross the site. People collect bits of wood or look for souvenirs from the once-grand hotel.

Inside the building workers throw debris down a huge chute, which leads into waiting trucks. Paul Starrett thought of the chute idea. You smile at how smart it is. It keeps debris off the streets. It also saves money on labor. Another worker hoses down the area with water to control the dust and dirt.

It gets dark, and you head home. Soon the world's tallest building will rise on the site of the old hotel, and you can't wait to see it happen. You've played a big role in the planning of the project, and you look forward to more projects that will come your way at Shreve, Lamb, and Harmon.

THE END

To follow another path, turn to page 11.
To read the conclusion, turn to page 101.

Cranes were positioned along the Waldorf-Astoria to demolish it as safely and efficiently as possible.

Skyscraper workers became known for their fearlessness as well as their hard work.

CHAPTER 3

WORKING IN THE SKY

The noise splits your ears. The sidewalk under your feet trembles as the huge construction machines roar all around. On the Empire State Building construction site, the first steel girders have gone up. One day all this noise and mess will end with the world's tallest building standing above New York's skyline.

The building isn't the biggest news in New York anymore. Last summer the city was buzzing with the news that rich investors were going to build the world's tallest building. But in October of 1929 the stock market crashed. This began the Great Depression. Soup kitchens opened around the city. Long lines of hungry people wait for hours to get food.

Turn the page.

Although almost every construction project in the city has shut down, construction on the Empire State Building has continued. You heard a rumor that some of the rich men who were building it weren't affected by the crash. That's good news for you. You come from a family of riveters—workers who connect steel girders to build structures such as skyscrapers. You, your father, uncle, and brother are very lucky. You all got jobs working on the Empire State. The pay is good, $1.92 an hour. That's more than a subway worker makes.

It's 8:00 a.m., time to be on the job. You arrived on time with your dad and brother. But your Uncle Tony is nowhere to be seen. The project construction superintendent, John Bowser, sees you and frowns.

"You know you have to work as a four-man team, or you don't work at all today," he grumbles. "Do you know how lucky you are to have a job? There are 10 men waiting to replace you if you can't do the work."

"He'll be here," your dad says.

Bowser looks at you. "My runner isn't here, either," he says. "You can work for me today."

To work as a runner, turn to page 46.

To wait for your uncle, turn to page 53.

You're not sure what a runner is, but you decide to give it a try. "You're the go-between with the owners, architects, builders, and all the subcontractors and foremen," Bowser says. "My usual guy is more of a secretary. He keeps track of contracts, payroll, and other paperwork. Today I need someone to run messages and deliver things around the construction site."

Bowser continues. "I need to know how much steel is going to be delivered today. I also need you to find out when the next shipment of limestone will arrive. And if you have time, find the timekeeper and bring me the list of the workers he hired today."

Alright, you think. *I'd better get started.*

You find the steel supervisor directing trucks loaded with steel girders as they arrive. The steel is so huge and heavy that the trucks must move very slowly. This way they won't damage the streets.

Huge cranes lift the steel girders off the trucks and high into the air. The building is already more than six stories high, so relay cranes sit on ledges on the higher floors. The girders are passed upward from crane to crane. At the top ironworkers carefully swing each girder into place. Then the riveters go to work, riveting the steel girders together.

The supervisor can barely hear you over the din of the construction. You ask again how much steel is going to be delivered today. He yells back, "Two stories' worth, same as yesterday and the day before. Tell the boss the steel looks good, the plant in Pittsburgh is doing a great job."

He asks if you could do him a quick favor. Someone needs to make sure all the steel girders have their numbers, and that they are in the right place.

To check the steel numbers for the supervisor, turn to page 48.

To stick with your list and check on the limestone order, turn to page 50.

Every steel girder has two numbers on it. One is the place where the girder will go in the skeleton of the building. The workers use this number to put the steel frame together quickly and efficiently.

The other number indicates the crane that will lift the girder into place. The workers match the numbers and send the steel to the right area of the site so the skeleton can go up quickly. The Pittsburgh steel mill is so good that it can make the steel and ship the girders to New York in less than a day. You place your hand on one of the newly delivered girders. The steel is so fresh that it still feels warm.

It looks like all the numbers are here and the girders are correctly placed, so you tell the supervisor. He thanks you for your help and sends you on your way.

Placing steel girders throughout the building's skeleton was similar to constructing a giant puzzle.

To check on the limestone order, turn to page 50.

To see if your uncle has arrived, turn to page 53.

The outside of the Empire State Building will be covered with slabs of limestone. As you watch, another truckload of limestone rumbles up the street and disappears into the building. You make a note to tell Mr. Bowser that his limestone shipment has already been delivered.

Inside, cranes lift the limestone off the trucks. The limestone goes into railcars that snake through the inside of the building. Several workers push a railcar of limestone to the area where it will be installed.

The supervisor is talking to someone as you approach. He introduces himself as Paul Starrett, the head contractor. Starrett often comes to the construction site to make sure things are going well.

"See that?" Starrett says. "Every slab of limestone is identical. They are all finished at the plant in Indiana. That way, we don't have piles of limestone sitting around waiting to be cut. That saves us a lot of time on this end. And we put all the cranes on the inside, instead of out on the street. There's no way anything will fall into a crowd."

You are amazed. You've never heard of a contractor who thought of so many details. No wonder they hired him for the job. You only have one item left on your list, but you wonder if you should check back in to see if your uncle has arrived.

To find the timekeeper, turn to page 52.

To check and see if your uncle has arrived, turn to page 53.

The timekeeper is the person in charge of hiring and paying workers. He greets you and hands you some papers to give to Bowser. "Only a few new hires today," he says. "We've got almost everyone we need now."

You remember what it was like when you were hired. All the hiring is done before 8:00 a.m., so you were here early. Your foreman gave you a hiring ticket with your name, how much you would be paid, and other information. The timekeeper put all that information on a card in his office.

You thank the timekeeper as you leave. You head off to find Mr. Bowser, happy to have completed everything on his list. You pick up the pace, hoping your family isn't waiting for you to get the day's work started.

Go to page 53.

Your dad and brother are ready to leave when your uncle appears, breathing hard from running. "Train accident," he gasps. "Am I too late?"

Bowser doesn't like it. "I should make you all leave," he says. "This job must be on time and we can't wait. Don't let it happen again."

You all nod, then head to the timekeeper's office. Everyone picks up their work numbers, etched on small brass disks. Each employee has one of these disks. When you come to work in the morning you pick up your disk. Someone comes around the job site twice a day, checking disks. Showing your disk at these times proves you're at the job. You also show your disk when you get paid on Friday. You slide your disk into your pocket, and then make your way to the worker elevators. These are four old elevators from the Waldorf-Astoria hotel, salvaged by the builders to save money.

Turn the page.

At the top floor you notice a hole in your pocket. Your brass disk is gone! You have to have it to get paid. The supervisor wants your team to get started, since you're late already. But you need to find that disk.

Once a red-hot rivet was pounded into place it would cool and expand, forming a solid bond between girders.

To get to work, go to page 55.

To retrace your steps, turn to page 59.

You decide to hope for the best and follow your team through the job site. Soon you are far above the street on the end of a steel girder.

Several riveting teams are working nearby. Each team has a heater, or passer, a catcher, a bucker-up, and a gunman. Your dad is the heater, in charge of heating up the rivets in the forge. The rivets get red-hot in the forge. Your job as catcher comes next. Your dad picks a rivet out of the fire with tongs and tosses it to you. You catch the red-hot rivet in a bucket. Then you pick up the rivet with a pair of tongs and push it into a hole in the steel plate. Your brother, the bucker-up, holds it in place while your uncle, the gunman, pounds the rivet into the hole with a riveting hammer. All this happens in less than a minute! Your team can pound more than 500 rivets during one workday.

Turn the page.

At noon everyone takes a break for lunch. As you eat your brother sits down beside you and holds out a disk. "Did you lose this? I found it by the elevator," he says. You slap him on the back, thanking him and feeling very lucky.

In the afternoon the sky darkens. A few raindrops fall. Your dad wants to stop working. Bad weather is dangerous. Rain can make the steel girders slick. Winds can blow a man off the girder. This weather doesn't look too bad, though. Maybe you can work through it.

To wait for the rain to stop, go to page 57.

To work through the weather, turn to page 60.

Your team decides not to take any chances. Everyone waits inside for the rain to stop. When it stops you head back out on the steel girders. Soon you and your team are moving together: throw, catch, place, hammer, throw, catch, place, hammer.

Just as you've found your rhythm, you slip on a patch of wet steel while positioning yourself to catch the next rivet. You catch yourself and avoid falling, but the rivet hits you in the head. You shake it off, laughing, showing off the burnt hair on your head.

The work starts up again, but you can't seem to focus. You miss two rivets in a row. Dad tells you to take a break, but you want to keep working.

57

To take a break, turn to page 58.

To keep working, turn to page 61.

After taking a break your head feels a lot better. When you get back on the steel, everything is fine. You work until 4:30 p.m., quitting time. The paymaster is making his rounds, surrounded by armed guards. He calls your name, and you show him your brass disk and number. He hands you an envelope filled with cash. Every worker gets paid this way.

Your brother whispers, "30th floor." That's where the workers will meet after the bosses have gone home. As the sun sets you make your way there. The men have set up makeshift card tables. You'd love to play cards, but you don't want to gamble away your paycheck. Maybe you should go home instead.

To go home, turn to page 63.

To stay with your brother, turn to page 64.

You tell the supervisor that you'll be right back. You head back to the elevators, scanning the floor. There's so much noise that you don't notice a railcar full of steel barreling down its track. It slams into you, throwing you several feet. You're barely conscious as several men carry your limp body to the first-aid shack. Your head will heal, but your work on the Empire State Building is finished.

The Chrysler Building is visible in the center of the skyline behind an Empire State riveting team.

THE END

To follow another path, turn to page 11.
To read the conclusion, turn to page 101.

Your team keeps working, even though all the other teams find shelter inside. The sky gets darker. You agree to pound one last rivet and go inside too. Your dad tosses the red-hot rivet to you, and you slip on a wet spot on the steel girder. Your brother grabs your arm as you go over the edge. You dangle there for a few seconds, nothing but air between you and death. Then your brother hauls you up with a jerk. Something snaps, sending a terrible pain shooting through your arm.

You lie there gasping as a crowd gathers. Your dad looks both angry and relieved. At the hospital the doctor sets your broken arm and gives you the bad news: no more work for six weeks. That means your family is out of work too.

THE END

To follow another path, turn to page 11.
To read the conclusion, turn to page 101.

You decide to keep working. You gulp down some water, wipe your head, and get back to work. Things are fine for a little while, but soon your head begins to pound. Finally you have to stop. Dad promises to get your paycheck for you. You stop at one of the nursing stations on the site. The kind nurse bandages the lump on your head and tells you to take it easy. Then you make it down to the street.

The crowds are thick, watching the workers high above. You stop and glance upward. The workers look like ants crawling around on the bare steel. Someone has set up a telescope in Bryant Park so people can watch the action. You don't need to see it up close.

By the time you get home you're feeling much better. Tomorrow you'll be back up there, one of the sky boys working on the Empire State Building.

Riveting crews had to do difficult jobs, often in awkward positions at dizzying heights.

THE END

To follow another path, turn to page 11.
To read the conclusion, turn to page 101.

You were never very good at cards anyway. You crowd onto the old Waldorf-Astoria hotel elevator and ride to the street. It's almost dark, but you can see the sunset over the city. The half-finished Empire State Building glows in the red-gold light. You stand there until the red sun disappears, then you make your way home.

You pass a handful of men begging on the street corner. You wish you could help them, but you know that you can't. Grateful as you are for your current job, it won't last much longer. After the Empire State Building is complete you might be standing on the street corner too, unemployed and begging. But for now you try to focus on good things. Monday you'll be back, ready to continue work on the world's tallest building.

THE END

To follow another path, turn to page 11.
To read the conclusion, turn to page 101.

You're not much of a card player, but you don't feel like going home. You hang around with the other men, laughing and swapping stories. Suddenly you hear a commotion at one of the card tables. Your brother is arguing angrily with another man.

You rush to your brother's side as the man takes a swing. He clips you on the chin and you go down. A brawl breaks out. Someone tries to hit you, but you grab him and throw him to the ground. The two of you wrestle on the floor for a few minutes until a foreman appears. He breaks up the fight and tells you all to go home. You head down to street level with your brother and some of the other workers. Your brother has a black eye and his nose is bleeding. Smiling, you offer him a rag to wipe his face.

On the journey home you think about your work. You hope that one day you'll look up at the Empire State Building and proudly tell people that you helped build it.

Empire State workers pause for a group portrait on the building's steel skeleton in 1931.

THE END

To follow another path, turn to page 11.
To read the conclusion, turn to page 101.

During its construction the Empire State Building rose at an average rate of 4.5 floors per week.

CHAPTER 4

THE EMPIRE STATE TAKES SHAPE

The first months of 1930 are rough for people in New York. The Great Depression is taking hold, and more people than ever are out of work. The newspapers keep saying things will get better soon, but you don't believe them anymore. Your father lost his job weeks ago.

It feels as though the only hopeful thing in the whole city is the Empire State Building. Every day it rises higher over New York. It's going up so fast that no one can believe it.

67

Turn the page.

Early one morning you're standing with the rest of the crowd, neck stretched upward, watching the ironworkers and riveters perch on the steel girders far above. They fearlessly swing, jump, walk, and crawl over the steel. You wonder what it would be like to work in the sky.

Several boys your age are heading to the construction site. Curious, you follow them. One tells you that water boys are needed for the construction. You follow the boys into the half-completed building. Someone directs you to the timekeeper's office. There's a line of men and boys already there, and it's not even 7:00 a.m.

To change your mind, go to page 69.

To go to the end of the line and wait, turn to page 71.

You have a terrible fear of heights. You shake your head, shivering at the thought of working up in the steel. Quietly you turn around and run home. You tell your dad that they are hiring workers on the Empire State Building, and he rushes to the site. You don't see him all day, but you don't dare hope.

It's dark when he gets home, carrying a small bag of groceries. You can tell from the relief in his eyes that he got a job.

Turn the page.

"It's not permanent, just a helper to clean up and remove debris," he says. "But it's honest work and I'm glad to have it." Together you prepare a pot of soup, the first decent meal you've had in weeks.

"We'll get by," he says. But later you feel badly that you didn't even try to get a job. The next morning you are determined to try again.

A New York charity feeds and houses the unemployed. Soup kitchens became common in the United States during the Great Depression.

To go to the job site, go to page 71.

To look for another job, turn to page 92.

You stand in line behind the rest of the job seekers. Soon a man appears and starts asking you questions.

"How old are you?" he asks.

"Fourteen," you reply.

"Have you ever worked construction before?" he continues. "Are you afraid of heights?"

You gulp, shaking your head.

The man looks at your thin coat and worn shoes. He writes something down on a piece of paper.

"You're hired," he says. "You're going to be a water boy. The timekeeper will tell you what to do."

Turn the page.

The timekeeper records your information in a large book, and then hands you a brass disk with a number.

"This is your number," he says. "Don't lose this disk. You need that number to get paid every Friday. Bring it back to me at the end of the day."

Your job is to take water to the workers all around the construction site. A foreman points you to the area where the other water boys fill their buckets.

"Better not be afraid of heights," one boy says. "Those sky boys up on the girders will toss you to the wind."

You don't really believe that anyone would throw you off the building, but you're not going to get too near the edge, either.

"Listen up," the foreman says. "I need water boys to take care of the bricklayers. I also need someone to head up to the top floors to the ironworkers." He hands you a list of workers and where they are located on the construction site.

To go to the bricklayers, turn to page 74.

To go to the ironworkers, turn to page 80.

You aren't sure where to go first. Someone tells you to head to the basement. When you get there, you're astonished to see two huge hoppers filled with bricks. There are large openings above the hoppers.

The workers thankfully gulp the water you brought and wipe the sweat off their faces. "I'll bet you've never seen the likes of this," one says. "No one has. It was Paul Starrett's idea." He tells you that Starrett is the head contractor on this job.

Another worker explains what is going on. "On a normal job, the bricks are dumped into piles. Men load the bricks into wheelbarrows and take them where they need to go."

Constructing the mooring mast at the top of the building was the final step to completing the Empire State's steel skeleton.

Turn the page.

"But not this job!" another man says. "Each of these hoppers can hold 20,000 bricks. The trucks drive right into the building and dump their bricks into those openings. The bricks fall down the openings into the hoppers. Each hopper has a small slot. The bricks go through a slot into dump cars. The dump cars hold about 400 bricks."

Once a floor's steel girders were in place, crews of bricklayers followed.

Several men push each dump car along a special rail track to a hoist. They're attached to the hoist, and then disappear upward.

"Those cars go right up to the floors where they are needed," another man says. "Those bricks won't be touched by human hands from the time they are made at the brickyard until they are put into a wall!"

The workmen thank you for the water and tell you the bricklayers are up on the 38th and 39th floors.

Turn to page 78.

The noise is as bad up here as it is down below. Hundreds of people are working: plasterers, electricians, concrete workers, helpers cleaning up debris, and many others. The bricklayers are working on the walls.

You've never seen bricklayers build a wall so fast, and with such care. The bricks make an inner wall that supports the limestone outer layer. Helpers pile bricks next to each bricklayer. All the bricklayers have to do is reach for a brick, put it in place, spread a layer of mortar, and reach for the next one.

One of the bricklayers comes over for a drink. "Did you know that we use 100,000 bricks every day?" he asks. "That's what it takes to build a floor a day. We're going to use 10 million before this job is over!"

You make sure the other thirsty bricklayers get a welcome drink from your water bucket. Now you need to get to other workers. But just then your stomach growls and you realize it's almost lunchtime.

To find the limestone workers, turn to page 86.

To get some lunch, turn to page 88.

The ironworkers are the workers who crawl to the edge of the steel girders. Sometimes they even eat lunch or take naps on a girder! You take a deep breath and go all the way to the top of the construction site.

Several men sit calmly at the edge of a girder while a huge crane gently lowers another girder to them. The men grab the girder with gloved hands and guide it into place. A few bolts lock it down until the riveting team can finish putting it together. After placing a girder the ironworkers fearlessly climb down and move to the next one.

A group of ironworkers spot you and come over for a welcome break. They're speaking a language you have never heard.

"We're Mohawks," a friendly young ironworker explains. "We're from Canada, and some of us drive to New York every week to work." He goes on to say that he rents an apartment in Brooklyn with many other Mohawks. They stay in the city all week, and then drive home on the weekends. But some workers like New York so much that they've moved their families here for good.

Turn the page.

He explains that Mohawks have worked on high-rise projects for years. Some people think they have a special ability to fearlessly walk on the steel. "I'm not sure about that," the young man says. Then he looks at you. "Want to learn how to walk on the steel? It feels like walking on air."

The workers who took on the most dangerous jobs walking on high steel girders came to be known as "skywalkers." They were famous for their fearlessness.

To refuse his offer, go to page 83.

To try to walk on the steel, turn to page 93.

You shake your head, terrified at the thought. The man shrugs. "It's not for everyone," he says. "We're careful, we know how dangerous the work is." He takes another drink from your bucket and scrambles back onto a girder, ready to place the next piece of steel.

You examine the foreman's list and realize that the carpenters should be the next workers you visit.

Turn to page 84.

Carpenters do many jobs. You see them on almost every floor. Mainly they build frameworks, temporary supports to hold up walls, and temporary flooring. You see a lot of carpenter helpers, because one of their jobs is taking care of the water barrels. They also keep the work areas clear of debris and help out in the storerooms.

You go to several floors, delivering water and refilling your bucket. Along the way you give water to many other workers. You meet electricians, plumbers, concrete mixers, hoist managers, elevator builders, glazers working on the glass windows, and dozens of others. You had no idea it took this many professions to build one building.

You notice that it's almost lunchtime. But you think you may have time to give water to the limestone workers before taking a break.

The speed of the Empire State Building's construction meant that many different types of work went on at once.

To look for the limestone workers, turn to page 86.

To get some lunch, turn to page 88.

You head down to the loading area. There, trucks loaded with crates of limestone rumble in. Each crate has a key that tells the loaders where it needs to go in the building. Electric hoists move along a monorail in the ceiling. Each hoist picks up a crate of limestone and swings it down the monorail to a railway car. The cars go to the right floor, taking the limestone where it should go.

The whole monorail system is amazing. Nothing like it has ever been used on another construction site. After the workers here get water, you head up to the floors where they are setting the limestone.

"The architects were really smart," one limestone worker says as he gets a drink. "They designed the building so that all the limestone slabs would be the same. Saves a bunch of money and time that way."

After making sure all the limestone workers have had a drink, you head off to get some lunch.

Some steel workers used a rivet heater to toast bread and warm coffee during their lunch breaks.

Turn to page 88.

Everyone on the site breaks for lunch at noon. Each worker gets 30 minutes to eat. That's not enough time for thousands of men to wait for an elevator, get down to the street, buy lunch, eat, and get back to work. So the builders got the idea to have restaurants inside the building.

You get in line at the lunch counter on the 24th floor. The menu includes chicken salad, beef stew, beefsteak pie, hot dogs, and drinks such as coffee, milk, and soda. You notice ice cream and candy on the menu too. The prices are a few cents lower than lunch stands on the street below.

To sit with other water boys nearby, go to page 89.

To eat alone, turn to page 94.

Everyone is talking about the new Chrysler Building, which is now the world's tallest skyscraper. During its construction, the builders had a secret. They had made a huge, needlelike spire for the top of the building. They didn't want anyone to know about it until the last minute. When the spire went on, the building was 1,046 feet tall.

"But the Empire State will beat it," one boy boasts. "Did you know they're building an airship mast on the top? Airships will dock on the top of the world! The mast will be taller than the spire on the Chrysler Building. We'll be the world's tallest."

Turn the page.

You've seen the huge, silver airships gliding over the city. What a wonder riding in one would be!

As the weeks fly by, you arrive at work early, stay late, and do as many extra jobs as you can. The Empire State keeps going up, up, up, almost a floor a day. Finally the huge silver airship mast is placed on the top. The Empire State becomes the world's tallest by 200 feet!

The building is done, and it's time for the grand dedication.

To go to the dedication, go to page 91.

To skip the dedication, turn to page 95.

On May 1, 1931, it feels like the carnival has come to town. The whole city is excited about the dedication. Macy's department store has a special display. The newspapers are filled with ads and articles about the Empire State. You join the crowds as they listen to Al Smith and Governor Franklin D. Roosevelt give speeches. Then President Herbert Hoover, all the way down in Washington, D.C., presses a button. The Empire State Building lights up!

"Let's go up to the observation deck," your dad says suddenly. "I've saved up a bit so we can buy tickets. It will be a celebration!"

You're surprised, but you can't help worrying about spending money in these hard times. Maybe it would be better to save the money for something else.

To go to the observation deck, turn to page 96.

To say no, turn to page 98.

No one is hiring. By the end of the day you are worn out and hungry. You think about your father's temporary cleaning job and shake your head. You know it won't put much food on the table. Your father often looks on the bright side. You know he needs you to find ways to make some money.

As you walk through a park on the way home, you spy a woman with a large purse. In a flash you grab the purse. Her screams echo behind you as you run. Unfortunately for you, a cop sees the whole thing and chases you down. He slaps cold handcuffs on your wrists and hauls you to the police station. You're too tired and depressed to fight. All you can think is that you'll have a hot meal and a warm place to sleep in jail.

THE END

To follow another path, turn to page 11.
To read the conclusion, turn to page 101.

The man tells you his name is Akash. He shows you how to walk with one foot in front of the other, slowly, to keep your balance. When you're ready, Akash ties a rope around your waist, "just in case," he says. With your heart pounding, you take a step out onto the steel, then another. There's nothing between you and the ground far below except air.

For a minute you feel like a bird soaring over this great city. This isn't scary—it's amazing! You're on top of the world, on top of the tallest building ever made. You'll never forget this moment.

THE END

To follow another path, turn to page 11.
To read the conclusion, turn to page 101.

You're finishing your milk when the foreman finds you. He has bad news. He's hired too many water boys, and you aren't needed. He hands you one day's pay even though you've only worked a few hours.

"I'm sorry," he says, shaking your hand. "Come back, though. I may need you next week."

Disappointed, you promise to come back. Hopefully he'll have room for you next week. At least this money will help buy your family food for a day or two.

THE END

To follow another path, turn to page 11.
To read the conclusion, turn to page 101.

The last day of work was sad. Many of the workers were there for more than a year. And each worker dreaded what loomed ahead now that the job was finished: unemployment. The Great Depression is getting worse. Most construction projects have shut down. The first day you're out of work, you get dressed and head down to the soup kitchen. At least you will always be able to say you helped to build the world's tallest building. But that won't buy you food in these hard times.

THE END

To follow another path, turn to page 11.
To read the conclusion, turn to page 101.

The grand marble lobby is amazing. The huge golden mural of the Empire State takes your breath away. Your dad is impressed too.

The elevator zips up so fast that your ears pop. You get to the observation deck and step out. You've seen the view before, but your dad gasps in wonder. You can see all the way to New Jersey and Long Island. The Statue of Liberty looks tiny in the distance.

The Empire State Building's opening celebration gave people their first chance to see the amazing views from the observation deck.

As you are gazing at the view, someone taps your shoulder. It's Paul Starrett, the contractor for the building. "I have a proposition for you, young man," he says.

Starrett has heard about your hard work on the job site. "I need an assistant in my office a few days a week," he says. "Would you like the job?"

"Yes!" you say instantly. You agree on a day to start, and then Starrett disappears into the crowd. You can't believe your good fortune. Now you really do feel like you're on top of the world!

THE END

To follow another path, turn to page 11.
To read the conclusion, turn to page 101.

"Let's use the money to celebrate another way," you say. "How about a nice dinner in a real restaurant?" At first your dad looks disappointed. But you're both sick of soup and bread for dinner. This will be a treat for you both. He smiles, and together you leave the party behind.

THE END

To follow another path, turn to page 11.
To read the conclusion, turn to page 101.

The Empire State Building remained the tallest skyscraper in the world for nearly 40 years.

The Empire State Building's airship mooring mast was the tallest ever designed. But mooring an airship to such a tall mast turned out to be very difficult. Less than a year after the building opened, the mast was converted for use as a TV and radio antenna.

CHAPTER 5

TALLEST IN THE WORLD

The Empire State Building was the world's tallest skyscraper from its completion until 1970. A lot has happened to the building during its lifetime.

When it was first finished, the Empire State Building sat empty. The Great Depression hit the country hard. Thousands of companies closed down and millions of people were out of work. No company wanted the office space. People started calling it the "Empty State Building."

As the United States began to recover from the Great Depression, companies began to move into the building. By the time World War II ended in 1945, the building was finally bringing in money.

This was good news for the men who owned the building. John Raskob had poured his fortune into keeping the building going. He almost lost everything. But he had faith that his building would make it, and it did. He had a magnificent office in the building until he died in 1950.

The Empire State Building became world famous in 1933 when the movie *King Kong* was released. In the film a giant ape climbs the building and fights off airplanes until he falls to his death.

In 1945 the pilot of a B-25 bomber airplane lost his bearings in thick fog over New York. Trying to navigate safely, he accidentally steered the aircraft toward the Empire State Building. By the time he saw the building, it was too late to avoid a collision. The plane crashed into the Empire State Building between the 78th and 80th floors. The pilot, two others aboard the plane, and 11 people in the building were killed in the accident.

Betty Lou Oliver, an elevator operator, was injured in the crash. Wanting to send her down for treatment, rescue workers placed her in an elevator they thought was undamaged. But the cables had been damaged in the crash and they snapped. Amazingly, Betty survived the 75-story fall to the bottom of the elevator shaft.

The Empire State has stood the test of time. Its classic Art Deco style is a feature that makes it one of the most iconic buildings in the city.

Despite its iconic status, some parts of the building deteriorated over time. The remarkable lobby, with its marble walls and gold murals, was not kept in perfect condition. The ceiling mural was covered and forgotten.

Several renovation projects began in 2009. The lobby was restored. The marble walls were fixed, and the amazing ceiling mural was remade. Today millions of people from around the world see it before taking an elevator ride to the observation deck to gaze down at the city.

When the World Trade Center was finished in 1974, the Empire State Building lost its title as world's tallest building. But it still stands today as a magnificent symbol of New York.

Only two of the building's floors were affected in the 1945 bomber crash.

TIMELINE

1893—Millionaire William Waldorf Astor builds the Waldorf hotel on the corner of 33rd Street and Fifth Avenue in New York City.

1897—The Astoria Hotel goes up on the corner of 34th Street and Fifth Avenue. It is later joined with the Waldorf to become the Waldorf-Astoria hotel.

1913—The Woolworth Building is completed and becomes the tallest skyscraper in the world.

1929—John Jacob Raskob, Al Smith, and others form the Empire State Building Corporation.

The Waldorf-Astoria hotel is torn down to make way for the Empire State Building.

October 29, 1929—The stock market crashes, setting off the Great Depression.

March 17, 1930—Construction begins on the Empire State Building.

April 1930—The Bank of Manhattan Trust Building at 40 Wall Street beats the Woolworth Building to become the world's tallest.

May 1930—The Chrysler Building opens, becoming the world's tallest skyscraper.

May 1, 1931—The Empire State Building opens. It becomes the world's tallest skyscraper.

1933—The film *King Kong* features a huge ape climbing the Empire State Building.

1945—A B-25 bomber crashes into the side of the Empire State Building in a thick fog. The accident kills the 3 people aboard the plane and 11 people in the building.

1970—The World Trade Center North Tower is completed, beating the Empire State Building's height record.

1983—A giant King Kong balloon is installed on the top of the Empire State Building. The balloon is part of a celebration of the 50th anniversary of the film *King Kong*.

2009-2011—Renovation projects help to restore and clean areas of the Empire State Building.

OTHER PATHS TO EXPLORE

In this book you've seen how the events of the past look different from three points of view. Perspectives on history are as varied as the people who lived it. Seeing history from many points of view is an important part of understanding it. Here are some ideas for other Empire State Building points of view to explore:

* The Empire State Building took one year and 45 days to build at a total cost of over $40 million. Compare the cost and time and labor it took to construct the Empire State Building to some more recent skyscraper projects throughout the world. How do they compare? (Integration of Knowledge and Ideas)

* Thousands of people lost their jobs during the Great Depression. Work on projects such as the Empire State Building became increasingly rare. Discuss some of the reasons why people might stay in the city. Would it be better to risk leaving home to find a better life somewhere else? Support your answer with examples from the text and other sources. (Key Ideas and Details)

READ MORE

Banting, Erinn, and Heather Kissock. *The Empire State Building*. New York: AV2 by Weigl, 2014.

Bullard, Lisa. *The Empire State Building*. Minneapolis: Lerner Publications Co., 2010.

Hurley, Michael. *The World's Most Amazing Skyscrapers*. Chicago: Raintree, 2012.

INTERNET SITES

FactHound offers a safe, fun way to find Internet sites related to this book. All of the sites on FactHound have been researched by our staff.

Here's all you do:

Visit *www.facthound.com*

Type in this code: 9781491404003

GLOSSARY

architect (AHR-ki-tekt)—a person who designs buildings and structures

Art Deco (ART DEK-oh)—an art style with bold geometric shapes and sharply defined outlines

charitable (CHAYR-uh-tuh-buhl)—done out of generosity

demolition (de-muh-LI-shuhn)—to tear down an object or building

hoist (HOIST)—a machine that can lift heavy objects

limestone (LIME-stohn)—a sedimentary rock used in building

monorail (MON-uh-rayl)—a railroad that runs on one rail, usually high above the ground

mural (MYUR-hul)—a large picture painted or attached to a wall or ceiling

rivet (RIV-it)—a metal pin that holds steel girders together

salvage (SAL-vij)—to save something

BIBLIOGRAPHY

Berman, John S. *The Empire State Building.* New York: Barnes and Noble Books, 2003.

Flowers, Benjamin Sitton. *Skyscraper: The Politics and Power of Building New York City in the Twentieth Century.* Philadelphia: University of Pennsylvania Press, 2009.

Kingwell, Mark. *Nearest Thing to Heaven: The Empire State Building and American Dreams.* New Haven, Conn.: Yale University Press, 2006.

Korom, Joseph J. *The American Skyscraper, 1850-1940: A Celebration of Height.* Boston: Branden Books, 2008.

Langmead, Donald. *Icons of American Architecture: From the Alamo to the World Trade Center.* Westport, Conn.: Greenwood Press, 2009.

Miller, Ron. *Seven Wonders of Engineering.* Minneapolis: Twenty-First Century Books, 2010.

Reis, Ronald A. *The Empire State Building.* New York: Chelsea House Publishers, 2009.

Roberts, Gerrylynn K. *American Cities & Technology: Wilderness to Wired City.* London; New York: Routledge in association with the Open University, 1999.

Tauranac, John. *The Empire State Building: The Making of a Landmark.* Ithaca, N.Y.: Cornell University Press, 2014.

Willis, Carol, ed. *Building the Empire State.* New York: W.W. Norton in association with the Skyscraper Museum, 1998.

INDEX